History of America
The First Fight
for Rights

1845 to 1928

Sally Senzell Isaacs

Heinemann
LIBRARY

First published in Great Britain by Heinemann Library,
Halley Court, Jordan Hill, Oxford OX2 8EJ,
a division of Reed Educational and Professional Publishing Ltd.
Heinemann is a registered trademark of Reed Educational & Professional
Publishing Limited.

OXFORD MELBOURNE AUCKLAND
JOHANNESBURG BLANTYRE GABORONE
IBADAN PORTSMOUTH NH (USA) CHICAGO

HISTORY OF AMERICA: THE FIRST FIGHT FOR RIGHTS
was produced for Heinemann Library by Bender Richardson White.

Editor: Lionel Bender
Designer: Ben White
Assistant Editor: Michael March
Picture Researcher: Pembroke Herbert and Nancy Carter
Media Conversion and Typesetting: MW Graphics
Production Controller: Kim Richardson

03 02 01 00 99
10 9 8 7 6 5 4 3 2 1

Printed in Hong Kong

British Library Cataloguing-in-Publication Data.
Isaacs, Sally Senzell
   The First Fight for Rights, 1845–1928. – (History of America)
   1. United States - History - 1901–1953 - Juvenile literature
   2. United States - History - 19th century - Juvenile literature
   I. Title.
   973.9'1

ISBN 0431 05630 7 Hb   ISBN 0431 05636 6 Pb

Acknowledgements
The producers of this book would like to thank the following for permission to
reproduce photographs:
Picture Research Consultants, Mass: pages 6 (Library of Congress),
8 (Seneca Falls Historical Society), 14bl (Library of Congress), 14cr (University of
Illinois at Chicago, The University Library, Jane Addams Memorial Collection),
16 (Yosemite Museum/Leroy Radanovich), 19b (Library of Congress/A.J.
Wingren), 23 (Smithsonian Institution), 26 (Archives of Labor and Urban Affairs,
Wayne State University), 27 (Library of Congress), 30 (Library of Congress),
32t (National Archives), 32b (Imperial War Museum, London), 35 (General
Electric), 38 and 39 (Smithsonian Institution). Peter Newark's American Pictures:
pages 7, 9, 10, 11, 12, 19t, 21, 22, 24, 28, 29, 31, 36, 40, 41. North Wind
Pictures: 13, 17, 20, 25. CORBIS: pages 34 (www.corbis.com/Bettmann),
37 (The National Archives).

Illustrations by: John James on pages 6/7, 8/9, 10/11, 18/19,
20/21, 22/23, 26/27, 30/31, 32/33, 40/41; Gerald Wood on pages 16/17,
24/25, 36/37, 38/39; James Field on pages 12/13, 14/15, 28/29, 34/35.
All maps by Stefan Chabluk.

Cover design and make-up by Pelican Graphics. Cover artwork by John James.
Photos: Top: Peter Newark's American Pictures. Centre: Picture
Research Consultants (Library of Congress). Bottom: Peter Newark's American
Pictures.

Every effort has been made to contact copyright holders of any material
reproduced in this book. Omissions will be rectified in subsequent printings if
notice is given to the publisher.

Special thanks to Mike Carpenter, Scott Westerfield and Tristan Boyer at
Heinemann Library for editorial and design guidance and direction.

For more information about Heinemann Library books, or to order, please phone
01865 888066, or send a fax to 01865 314091. You can visit our web site at
www.heinemann.co.uk

Any words appearing in the text in bold, **like this**, are
explained in the Glossary.

Major quotations used in this book come from the
following sources. Some of the quotations have been
abridged for clarity.
Pages 9 and 10: Elizabeth Cady Stanton and Susan B.
Anthony speeches: From *Elizabeth Cady Stanton-Susan B.
Anthony: Correspondence, Writings, Speeches.* New York:
Schocken Books, 1918, page 31.
Page 16: Elinore Rupert Stewart letter: From: *A History of
US: An Age of Extremes* by Joy Hakim. New York: Oxford
University Press, 1994, page 106.
Page 17: Anna Howard Shaw quote: From *Elizabeth Cady
Stanton-Susan B. Anthony: Correspondence, Writings,
Speeches.* New York: Schocken Books, 1918, pages
219-220.
Page 20: Jack London's quote: From *Eyewitness to
America,* edited by David Colbert. New York: Pantheon
Books, 1997, page 315.
Page 28: New York observer quote: From *Discovering
America's Past.* Pleasantville, NY: Reader's Digest, 1993,
page 222.
Page 36: Paul Morand quote: From *Eyewitness to
America,* edited by David Colbert. New York: Pantheon
Books, 1977, page 363.
Page 38: Woodrow Wilson's speech: From *Let Women
Vote* by Marlene Targ Brill. Brookfield, Connecticut: The
Millbrook Press, 1996, page 50.
Page 38: William Taft quote: From *Women's Rights* by
Janet Stevenson. New York: Franklin Watts, Inc., 1972,
page 62.
Page 39: Carrie Chapman Catt quote: From *The Story of
the Nineteenth Amendment* by R. Conrad Stein, Chicago:
Childrens Press, 1982, page 31.

The Consultants
Special thanks to Diane Smolinski, Nancy Cope
and Christopher Gibb for their help in the
preparation of this book.

CONTENTS

History of America is a series of nine books arranged chronologically, meaning that events are described in the order in which they happened. However, each book focuses on an important person in American history, so the timespans of the titles overlap. In each book, most articles deal with a particular event or part of American history. Others deal with aspects of everyday life, such as trade, houses, clothing and farming. These general articles cover longer periods of time. The little illustrations at the top left of each article are a symbol of the times. They are identified on page 3.

▼ **About the map**

This map shows the United States today. It shows the boundaries and names of all the states. Refer to this map, or to the one on pages 42–43, to locate places talked about in this book.

About this book

This book is about America from 1845 to 1928. The term America means 'the United States of America', also called the US. Many important events happened in America during this time period, including the Civil War and the Native American struggle. Although they are mentioned in this book, these two topics are the subjects of two other books in this series. This book focuses on social issues such as the African-American experience, the growth of cities and industry, and the fight for women's voting rights. Words in **bold** are described in more detail in the Glossary on page 46.

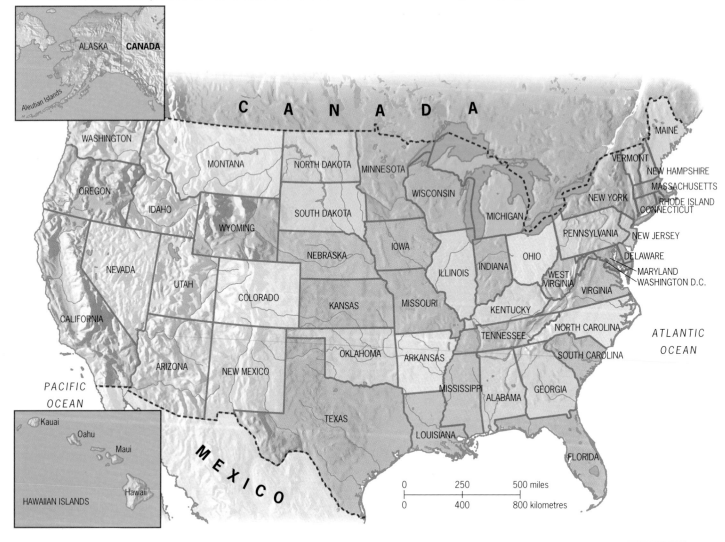

INTRODUCTION

In 1845, most Americans lived on farms. They grew their own food and made their own clothes. More than four million African Americans were **slaves** in the South. Big changes were ahead.

Between 1861 and 1865, the nation split apart. Arguments flared between leaders in the northern and southern states over slavery and other issues. Finally a **civil war** broke out. For the only time in history, Northerners and Southerners killed each other on American soil. When the war ended, the states reunited under one government. Slavery was outlawed. African Americans began their struggle to get jobs, an education and equal opportunities.

For many years after the Civil War, most women in the US did not have **suffrage**, which is the right to vote. In a country that had fought for freedom and individual rights, women did not have a voice in their government. Achieving that was the lifetime goal of Susan B. Anthony. She helped women to win that right in 1920.

By 1920, most Americans had moved to cities. They travelled in trains and even cars. Daring men and women took flying machines into the sky. American factories and steel **mills** made most of the world's products. American women and men made their country into one of the strongest in the world. Many events in this book took place during Susan B. Anthony's life. Other events happened after she died. On pages that describe events during Anthony's life, there are yellow boxes that tell you what she was doing at the time.

LESSONS IN EQUALITY

Today in the US, women can be judges, governors and company presidents. They can run businesses, meetings and election campaigns. In 1845, none of this was possible. Most men and women believed women were not smart enough for these jobs. They believed women should work quietly at home.

As Susan Brownell Anthony grew up, she knew girls were treated differently from boys. In her school in Battenville, New York, girls sat at the back of the classroom. Often the teacher taught challenging lessons to the boys in the front. Susan was frustrated because she could not hear the lessons. Luckily, Susan's parents did not accept such inequality.

Susan's family belonged to the Quaker Church, also known as The Society of Friends. This Church was founded by William Penn, an Englishman, in 1662. The state of Pennsylvania is named after him. Quakers believed in equality for all and in giving children a good education. Susan's father encouraged everyone to voice their opinions. When he saw that the girls were not getting an equal education, he built his own small school beside his house and cotton **mill**. His children, as well as the children of the mill workers, went to the school. There, teachers treated boys and girls the same.

▼ This is a newspaper that spoke out against **slavery.** In the South, African American slaves were forced to work with no pay and no freedom. People, like Susan and her parents, who wanted to end slavery were called abolitionists. Abolitionists frequently gathered at the Anthony house in Rochester, New York.

Facts about Susan
Born on 15 February 1820 in Adams, Massachusetts.
Moved to New York State in 1826
Father: Daniel Anthony
Mother: Lucy Read Anthony
Brothers and sisters: Guelma, Hannah, Daniel, Mary, Eliza, Merritt
First jobs: worker in father's mill, age 12; private tutor for a family, age 16; teacher in a school, age 20
Because they were Quakers, the family lived a simple life. They dressed in plain clothes, and rarely played games, danced or listened to music.

▶ Canajoharie Academy was similar to a private school today. Susan taught reading, spelling, writing, maths, science, philosophy and history in the girls' department. She took her students on field trips, played games with them, and helped them put on plays.

Susan becomes a teacher

In 1840, at the age of 20, Susan became a teacher in New Rochelle, New York State. She replaced a male teacher who earned $10 a week. Susan was paid only $2.50 a week because she was a woman. Still, Susan earned her own money. Most women in 1840 felt they must get married so that a husband could support them.

In 1846, Susan became the headmistress for the 'female department' of Canajoharie Academy in northern New York State. It was a very important job. Her students and their parents thought she was a wonderful teacher. Susan now lived away from her family. She first lived with her uncle Joshua, and later with her cousin Margaret.

▼ This is the music book for an **anti-slavery** song written by Jesse Hutchinson Jr in 1845. It was written to honour Frederick Douglass, a former slave who became an anti-slavery leader. He lived in Rochester and frequently attended abolitionist meetings at the home of Susan's parents.

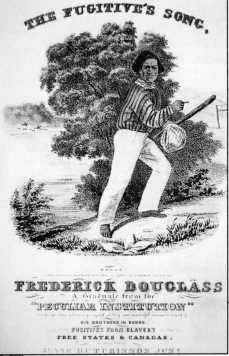

TIME FOR CHANGE

Many people wanted things to change in America. Some people wanted to outlaw alcohol because people who drank too much were dangerous. Some people wanted all slaves to be free. And some people wanted women to have the same rights as men.

Susan B. Anthony wanted all these things. She joined the **temperance movement** – people who wanted to stop the sale and use of alcoholic beverages. In 1852, she attended a meeting of the Sons of Temperance in Albany, New York State. At one point, she rose to give her opinion. A man jumped up and told her that women were not invited to speak. Anthony was furious. She stormed out of the room. Other women followed her. Now, she realized that there were other women who agreed with her and were willing to speak up for their rights.

▶ **Protest** marches like this one got everyone's attention. This picture shows a temperance march in front of an off-license. Many women wanted to outlaw alcohol because many husbands got drunk and beat their wives or lost their jobs.

▼ Those women who had jobs in factories or as teachers were poorly paid. Their earnings belonged to their husbands.

▼ In southern states, people were allowed to own **slaves**. Slaves had no rights. Slavery ended after the **Civil War** in 1865.

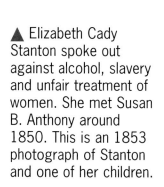

▲ Elizabeth Cady Stanton spoke out against alcohol, slavery and unfair treatment of women. She met Susan B. Anthony around 1850. This is an 1853 photograph of Stanton and one of her children.

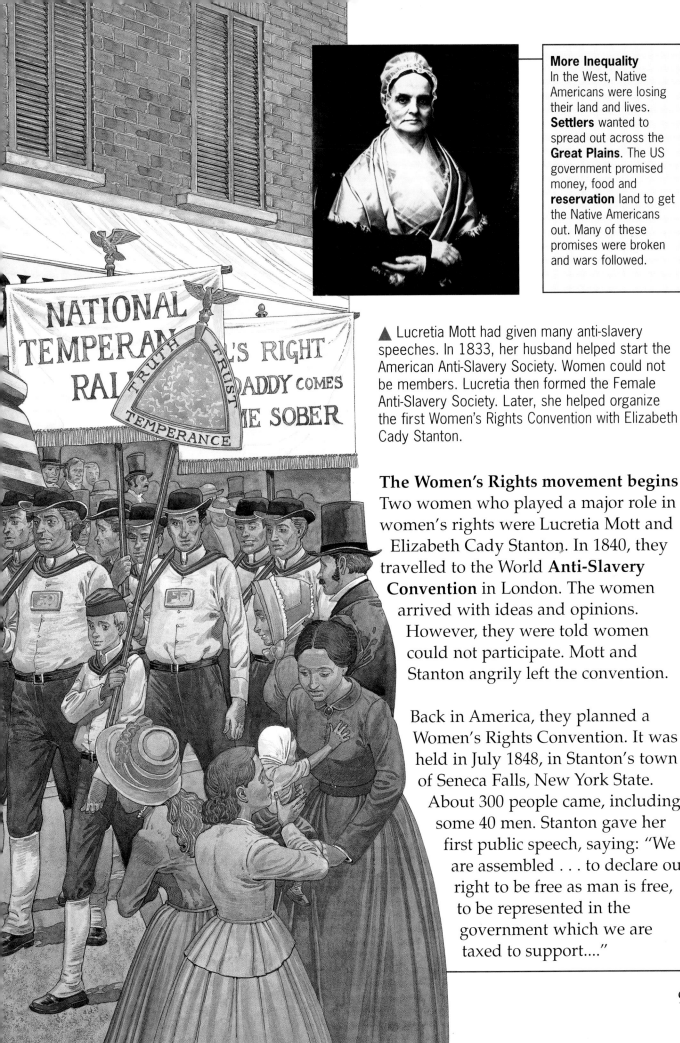

▲ Lucretia Mott had given many anti-slavery speeches. In 1833, her husband helped start the American Anti-Slavery Society. Women could not be members. Lucretia then formed the Female Anti-Slavery Society. Later, she helped organize the first Women's Rights Convention with Elizabeth Cady Stanton.

The Women's Rights movement begins

Two women who played a major role in women's rights were Lucretia Mott and Elizabeth Cady Stanton. In 1840, they travelled to the World **Anti-Slavery Convention** in London. The women arrived with ideas and opinions. However, they were told women could not participate. Mott and Stanton angrily left the convention.

Back in America, they planned a Women's Rights Convention. It was held in July 1848, in Stanton's town of Seneca Falls, New York State. About 300 people came, including some 40 men. Stanton gave her first public speech, saying: "We are assembled . . . to declare our right to be free as man is free, to be represented in the government which we are taxed to support...."

9

AN UPHILL BATTLE

"Friends and fellow-citizens: I stand before you for the crime of having voted at the last presidential election...but instead I simply exercised my citizen's right guaranteed to me and all United States citizens by the Constitution." Susan B. Anthony made this speech in 1872 after she was arrested for voting.

The lawmakers in each state made laws about who could vote. Before 1807, a few states allowed women to vote. After that year, no state allowed it. The US **Constitution** had power over the state laws. Before 1868, it said nothing about who could vote. In 1868, the 14th **Amendment** was added to the US Constitution. The amendment said all people born in the United States were legal citizens.

After the Civil War and slavery ends

In 1870, the 15th Amendment was passed. It said a person could not be denied the right to vote because of race, colour or 'previous condition of servitude'. African Americans, including former **slaves**, now had the right to vote.

Susan B. Anthony believed she was guaranteed the right to vote by the 14th Amendment. She was a legal citizen. She put the Constitution to a test. On 5 November 1872, she cast a vote in the presidential **election**. A few weeks later, she was arrested for breaking the law.

At her trial on 17 June 1873, the judge proclaimed Anthony guilty and fined her $100. "I shall never pay a dollar of your unjust penalty, " she said. The judge took it no further. He knew if he imprisoned her, she could take her case to the US **Supreme Court** and possibly win there.

▼ Anthony and Stanton believed women should be able to own **property**. Starting in 1854, they went from house to house asking people to sign a **petition**. They got 1000 signatures in the first year. They took the petition to New York's lawmakers. In 1860, the women succeeded in getting the state's property laws changed.

▲ In 1869, the women in Wyoming **Territory** were allowed to vote. When Wyoming became a state in 1890, it was the first state to allow women to vote.

▼ In the 1871 and 1872 elections, 150 women in 10 states tried to vote. Like Anthony, they were arrested and found guilty their trials.

▼ Victoria Woodhull was the first woman to speak before the US **Congress** about women's rights. In January 1871, she argued that the 14th and 15th Amendments gave women the right to vote. It was this speech that inspired Susan B. Anthony and other women to try to vote in the 1871 and 1872 elections.

▼ After she was arrested, Susan B. Anthony was not put in jail. She was released on **bail** until her trial. She spent the next few months giving speeches throughout New York State. She wanted to make people aware of the importance of women's rights. Her speech was called "Is it a Crime for a United States Citizen to Vote?"

Voting rights for African Americans
African American **slaves** in the South won their freedom in 1865. In 1870, African American men gained the right to vote. Here is a chronicle of events:
1861 Civil War begins
1863 President Lincoln declares all slaves in the warring southern states free (Emancipation Proclamation)
1865 Civil War ends
1865 the 13th Amendment makes slavery illegal in the US
1868 the 14th Amendment makes all people born in the US legal citizens
1870 the 15th Amendment guarantees African American men the right to vote

AMERICA'S RICH PEOPLE

The end of the 1800s were hopeful times for many Americans. Susan B. Anthony's speeches gave hope to women. Many Americans grew rich by owning steel mills and railways. Inventions such as electric lights and cars promised wonderful things for the future.

By 1890, one out of three Americans lived in a city. Cities had museums, theatres, department stores and sports arenas. Cities had telephones and electric lights. People travelled through cities on electric-powered tramcars.

During these years, many owners of businesses and shops became rich. In the 1880s, Chicago had 200 millionaires living in huge mansions along the shore of Lake Michigan. They filled their homes with expensive furniture, curtains and carpets, and with priceless artworks.

The Gilded Age

The American writer Mark Twain was concerned about these years. In 1873, he wrote a book called *'The Gilded Age.'*. Twain thought Americans were too interested in money and possessions. The book made fun of selfishness and money-making schemes.

Of course, most Americans were not rich. Many lived in crowded city buildings with little food or money. Young children wore clothes handed down from older brothers and sisters. Workers in steel mills and factories earned low wages. They often worked with dangerous machines and among poisonous fumes.

▼ This is the street called Broadway in New York City. In 1880, telephone and telegraph wires criss-crossed the street between poles.

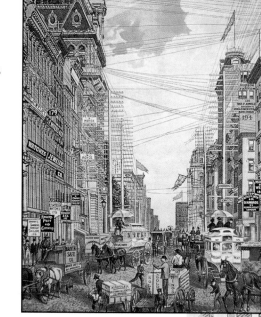

Equal Rights
During this time, Susan B. Anthony lived with her sister Mary in a middle-class house in Rochester, New York State. Between 1868 and 1870, she and Elizabeth Cady Stanton published a newspaper about equal rights. It was called '***Revolution***'.

◀ New inventions changed the lives of women. Many women took jobs as telephone operators (far left). With the first telephones, a person called an operator connected wires on the switchboard to put the call through. Other women took typing jobs in offices (left). The typewriter was invented in 1868.

◀ Shopping in a department store in the 1880s was very exciting. When the lift, or elevator, was first invented in 1857, people were afraid to enter them. In the 1880s, companies such as Woolworth started.

▲ This is a 1890s photograph of Fifth Avenue in New York City. The city's wealthiest people and smartest stores are still on Fifth Avenue.

◀ This wealthy family in New York City had many luxuries. These children are enjoying a birthday party in a spacious dining room with several servants.

HOMES FOR THE POOR

Anthony Amendment
Susan B. Anthony was concerned about poor working and living conditions. She felt if women had the right to vote, they could change the laws to make things better. In 1878, she convinced lawmakers in **Congress** to introduce an **amendment** about women's voting rights to the Constitution. It was called the Anthony Amendment. It was accepted in 1920.

"We cannot all live in the city, yet nearly all of us seem determined to do so," said newspaper editor Horace Greeley. Builders could not put up houses fast enough for all the people moving to the cities. Cities did not have enough clean water or means to handle all the rubbish.

Cities were becoming overcrowded. People with well-paid jobs, such as doctors, lawyers, office workers and skilled craftworkers, lived comfortably.

Factory workers, household workers and unskilled workers were suffering. They had to work between 12 and 14 hours a day, six or seven days a week. They earned low wages. Women, **immigrants**, and African Americans were given the lowest-paid jobs.

Poor people lived in crowded, run-down buildings, called **tenements**. Many of these buildings had no windows or heat. The streets were jammed with people, pushcarts and rubbish.

▲ In 1889, a Chicago woman named Jane Addams wanted to help poor women and children. She turned an old mansion into a **settlement house**. Volunteers helped her care for children while mothers worked. They also taught English to immigrants.

◀ Starting in 1892, most immigrants to America came through **Ellis Island** near New York City. Inspectors examined them before permitting them into the country, as in this photograph of the time.

▲ People in tenements got their washing and cooking water through pumps like this one. Several families shared the use of each pump.

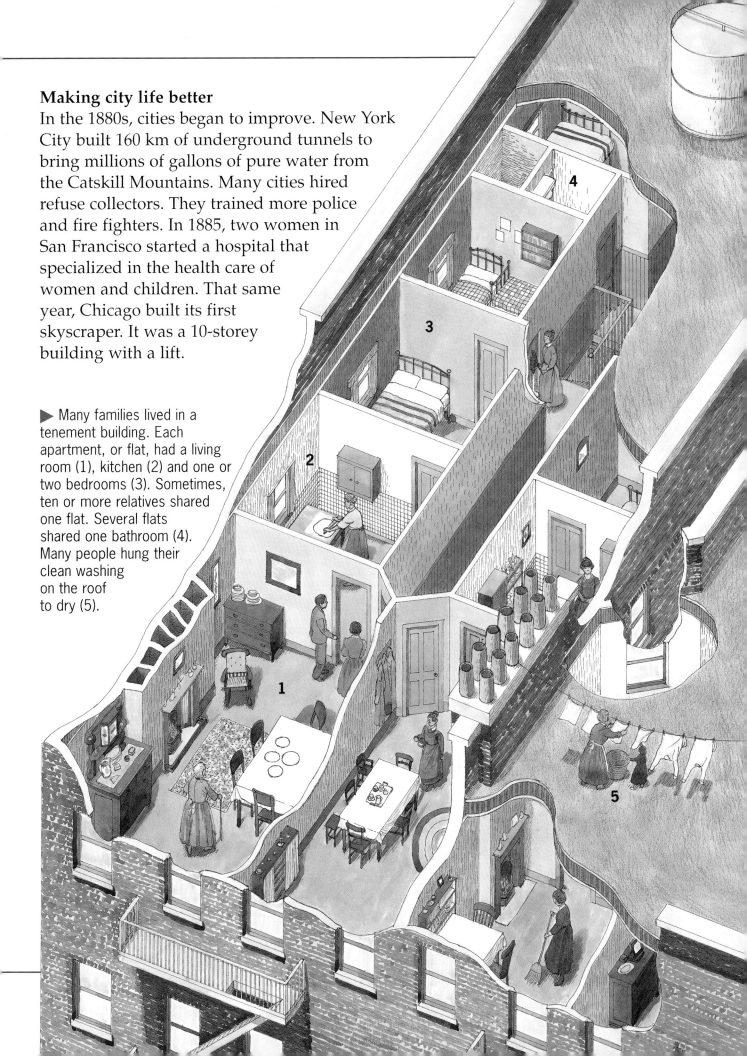

Making city life better

In the 1880s, cities began to improve. New York City built 160 km of underground tunnels to bring millions of gallons of pure water from the Catskill Mountains. Many cities hired refuse collectors. They trained more police and fire fighters. In 1885, two women in San Francisco started a hospital that specialized in the health care of women and children. That same year, Chicago built its first skyscraper. It was a 10-storey building with a lift.

▶ Many families lived in a tenement building. Each apartment, or flat, had a living room (1), kitchen (2) and one or two bedrooms (3). Sometimes, ten or more relatives shared one flat. Several flats shared one bathroom (4). Many people hung their clean washing on the roof to dry (5).

SETTLING MORE LAND

Tired of city problems, some people packed up and moved west to the open spaces of the Great Plains. This land once belonged to Native Americans. But since 1862, the US government made the Native Americans leave and encouraged settlers to go there.

The government offered land to anyone who had the courage to move west. These people were called homesteaders. Their lives were not easy. Planting crops was hard work. Troublesome pests and harsh weather were common.

Many homesteaders agreed with Elinore Rupert Stewart, who wrote: "To me, homesteading is the solution of all poverty's problems (although) persons afraid of coyotes and work and loneliness had better let ranching alone."

▶ In 1885, the government bought back land it had given the Native Americans in western Oklahoma. It offered the land to **settlers**. On 22 April 1889, nearly 100,000 people rushed into Oklahoma to **claim** land for their new homes.

▼ In 1890, **Congress** created Yosemite National Park in California to protect this beautiful land from development. This photo shows President Theodore Roosevelt and John Muir, a conservationist, at Yosemite in 1903.

Westward growth
1830 Congress passes the Indian Removal Act, forcing all Native Americans to live west of the Mississippi River
1845 Texas becomes part of the US
1846 US gets southern part of Oregon from Britain
1846-1848 US gets California and the South-west after war with Mexico
1848-1849 California gold rush
1862 The Homestead Act promises free land to settlers in the West
1869 transcontinental railway is completed
1890 Native Americans are killed at Wounded Knee Creek, South Dakota, the last Native American struggle to keep their land

▶ The Spanish–American War was fought in 1898. The US wanted to help Cuba win independence from Spain. First, the US attacked Spanish ships in the Philippine Islands in the Pacific Ocean, as shown in this picture. The war lasted four months. Cuba won independence.

▲ Before he became president in 1901, Theodore Roosevelt fought in the Spanish–American War. Roosevelt led fighting troops in Cuba. They were called Rough Riders.

▶ After the Spanish–American War, the US took over the Philippines, Puerto Rico and the island of Guam in the Pacific Ocean.

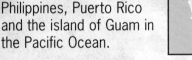

African American settlers

More than a half million people had settled in the **Great Plains** by 1898. Thousands of them were African Americans. They wanted to get far away from the South, where they had once been **slaves**. In the 1880s and 1890s, nearly 25,000 African Americans moved to Kansas. They called themselves Exodusters. They created the name from the book of *Exodus* in the Bible, which tells about Jews escaping slavery in Egypt.

The last frontier

Until this time, America always had a frontier – wide-open land not yet settled into towns. In 1890, the US government declared there was no more frontier. Over the previous 100 years, explorers, **pioneers** and **immigrants** had built communities throughout the country.

AFRICAN AMERICANS IN THE NEW SOUTH

Although slavery ended in 1865, many white people did not change their thinking about African Americans. They did not want to see African Americans get jobs and education. However, people such as Booker T. Washington gave African Americans opportunities and courage to succeed.

▼ Booker T. Washington was born a **slave** in Virginia. He was nine years old when slavery ended. After graduating from an African American college, he helped start Tuskegee Institute in 1881.

▼ Tuskegee Institute was a school for African American students in Alabama. One of its most famous teachers was George Washington Carver. In his experiments, he developed 300 uses for peanuts, including peanut butter.

Difficult times

African Americans worked hard at their jobs. Still they were paid less than white people. They were not offered highly paid jobs. Instead, they got dangerous or unpleasant jobs, such as cutting trees, digging sewers and cleaning streets. Women were the lowest paid of all. Many cleaned houses and worked in laundries.

Jim Crow laws

Lawmakers in the South passed laws to keep African Americans separated from white people. The laws were called Jim Crow laws. They said African Americans had to ride in separate railway carriages and tramcars. They had to enter factories through separate doors. They had to use a separate drinking fountain and sit in their own section of a theatre.

Losing the vote

African American men won the right to vote in 1870. In the 1890s, many states passed laws to keep them from voting. One law made voters pay a $2 poll tax. For many poor people, this was a week's wages. Another law made voters pass a reading test. No matter how well an African American man read, the tester almost always failed him.

▲ By 1906, Tuskegee Institute had 1500 students and a staff of 155. This is an algebra class at the Institute. Booker T. Washington wanted the students to learn not only maths and science but also such skills as building, farming and cooking. Some people criticized Washington for teaching skills that might keep African Americans in lower-paid jobs.

▼ Native American children were sent to government schools, as in this photograph from about 1900 at Swinomish **Reservation**, Washington.

▲ Government schools were supposed to 'Americanize' Native Americans. Children at the schools were encouraged to not wear traditional clothes (above left) but to dress like white Americans (above right). They were not allowed to use their Native American languages. Like African Americans, they could not vote.

DISASTERS

By 1900, Americans were feeling confident. American factories produced more goods than any other nation. Skyscrapers, rapid transport and electricity made cities more fantastic than ever. Anything seemed possible. No one expected any disasters.

"San Francisco is gone! Nothing remains of it but memories and a fringe of dwelling houses on the outskirts of town. The factories, the great stores and newspaper buildings, the hotels and palaces of the nabobs (rich people), are all gone.... On Wednesday morning at a quarter-past five came the earthquake. A minute later the flames were leaping upward.... The streets were humped into ridges and piled with debris of fallen walls. The steel rails were twisted. The telephone and telegraph systems were disrupted. And the great water mains had burst. All the shrewd contrivances (plans) and safeguards of man had been thrown out of gear by thirty seconds' twitching of the Earth's crust."

Jack London, a world-famous writer, wrote those words from San Francisco on 18 April 1906. That day, an earthquake, one of America's worst disasters, struck. The nation was shocked.

▶ Another disaster struck on 6 September 1901. President William McKinley was shot while visiting a world's fair in Buffalo, New York State. As he shook hands with the crowd of citizens, a man approached him. The man had a gun hidden under a bandage wrapped around his hand. McKinley died eight days later. Vice-president Theodore Roosevelt became the new president.

Women can vote
Susan B. Anthony died of pneumonia on 13 March 1906 at the age of 86. As she grew older, she encouraged younger women to continue to fight for women's **suffrage**. Women in Wyoming Territory were voting in 1869. In 1910, the state of Washington gave women voting rights. California followed in 1911, and Arizona, Oregon and Kansas in 1912.

▼ About 250,000 people lost their homes because of the San Francisco earthquake.

◄ The *Titanic* was built in Britain. It was called a 'floating palace' and thought to be unsinkable. In 1912, many famous people rushed to travel first-class on the ship's first voyage from England to New York City. Hundreds of poorer people travelled in the lower decks. On 14 April, the ship struck an iceberg and sank. About 700 people survived the disaster. About 1500 people died.

A city in flames

The earthquake lasted about 90 seconds. Then fires broke out as stoves and gas lamps overturned, electric wires broke and gas lines exploded. Fire fighters were nearly helpless because the water pipes had shattered. It took three days for the fires to die down. Nearly 30,000 buildings were destroyed. Over 500 people died. Citizens worked quickly to rebuild San Francisco. Ten years later, the city was thriving again.

NEW IDEAS IN A NEW CENTURY

More new ideas
1900 people buy the first personal camera, a Kodak Brownie, for $1 and can take pictures whenever they want
1903 the Boston Red Stockings (later Red Sox) beat the Pittsburgh Pirates in baseball's first World Series
1904 ice cream cones are first served at the St Louis World's Fair

Could the 1900s possibly bring as many changes as the 1800s? The new century opened with some extraordinary events. Two brothers from Ohio flew a machine into the air over North Carolina. A man in Michigan found a way for the average American to own a car.

Before the 1900s, inventors in Europe and America tried to create a good 'horseless carriage'. It was powered by a steam engine or battery. By 1900, some of them ran on petrol engines. Cars cost over $1000. Only rich people bought them.

In 1903, Henry Ford started the Ford Motor Company in Michigan. In 1912, workers assembled a car in about 12½ hours. Cars cost $825 each. Ford knew if he made cars faster, he could charge less money and average citizens could afford them. He created an assembly-line system in his factory. By 1914, his workers made a car in 1½ hours. By 1924, the cost of a car dropped to $290 and one out of every five Americans owned a car.

▲ America's first underground system was built in Boston in 1897.

▶ In Ford's factory, workers stood by a moving conveyor belt. The car parts moved in front of the workers. Each worker made or added one part of the car.

22

◀ On their first successful flight, Orville stretched out on the wing while Wilbur ran beside him. The plane stayed in the air for 17 seconds. Then Wilbur took a turn.

Wright Brothers take flight

Orville and Wilbur Wright dreamed of building a flying machine. On 17 December 1903, they made their dream come true. Weather experts helped them choose a beach near Kitty Hawk, North Carolina, for their first flight. The brothers flew their plane four times that day. The longest flight lasted 59 seconds. Only one newspaper wrote about it. In 1908, they flew before a large crowd in Virginia. These people were astonished. The Wright Brothers became famous.

▲ This photograph was taken around 1910. Early cars broke down often. Drivers pulled wires and turned handles, trying to restart the engine.

◀ Many businesses prospered because of the car. Factories making steel, glass, rubber and tools grew. New roadside restaurants opened. At first, people bought petrol in cans from shops. In 1913, a drive-in petrol station opened in Pittsburgh.

FARMING

America had once been a land of farmers. Even in 1860, five out of every six people lived on a farm. This was not true in 1913. Many Americans had left their farms for city jobs. Those who stayed on farms tried to make a business of it.

Some farmers still grew just enough food to feed their families. However, most farmers planted wheat, cotton or corn in large fields and sold their produce to merchants all over the country or in other parts of the world.

This kind of farming was costly. Farmers needed expensive machines. They also had to pay the railways to transport the crops. Farmers grew plenty of crops, but the huge supply drove down the prices. Many farmers lost their farms because they could not pay their expenses.

▼ Trains carried wheat and other farm products across the country. This is a train from the Santa Fe Railroad speeding through Crozier Canyon, Arizona, in 1910.

► By 1900, farmers on the **Great Plains** supplied much of the wheat used around the world. Some farmers used steam-powered tractors.

▼ This farmer needs 33 horses to pull his plough. His family is joining him for a picnic-lunch break.

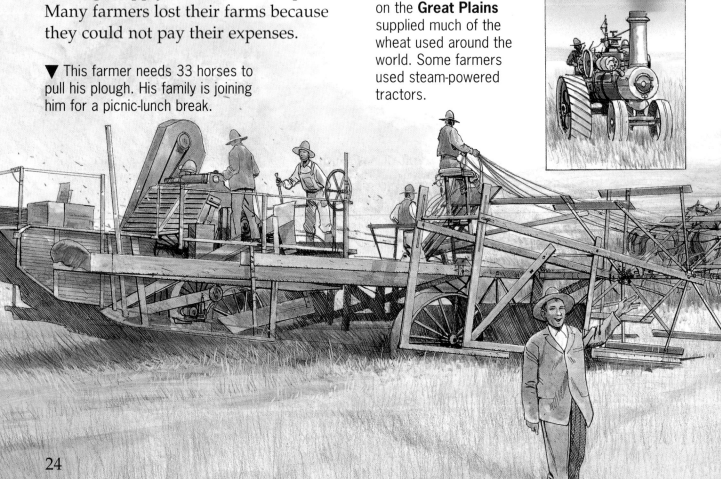

◀ Although they lived far from any shops, farm families could order almost anything from the Sears, Roebuck catalogue. In 1908, you could order this house to be delivered (unassembled) for $725 – about £4000 at today's prices.

◀ The cover of this pamphlet advertises a range of farm equipment that could be purchased from J.F. Seiberling and Co. The pamphlet was produced in about 1890 and was sent to local farmers.

Coping with problems

A group of people wanted to help farmers. They organized the National Grange in the late 1800s. Grangers helped farmers get together in **cooperative** groups. The groups could order seeds and tools in large quantities at lower prices. Grangers also built cooperative warehouses so that farmers could store their grain cheaply. Even with these efforts, many farmers could not make enough money.

In addition to money worries, farming families often felt lonely. The nearest neighbour might be more than 2 km away. Farming families tried to socialize whenever they could. They held picnics, dances and get-togethers to build houses or sew quilts.

INDUSTRY AND UNIONS

By 1914, America produced many of the world's products. There were several reasons for this: First, America had many natural resources, such as iron and coal. Second, America's railway system could take goods to distant places. Third, America had plenty of people to work in its mines and factories.

Industrial growth
Many cities became centres of industry:
- Birmingham, Alabama, and Pittsburgh, Pennsylvania – steel
- Milwaukee, Wisconsin – beer
- Detroit, Michigan – cars
- Minneapolis and St Paul, Minnesota – flour
- Kansas City, Missouri – meat-packing

America also had shrewd business leaders. Andrew Carnegie was one such leader. He built a steel company in Pennsylvania by using the best machinery and paying his workers low wages. He earned millions of dollars. After selling his business in 1901, Carnegie gave away over $324 million to build colleges, libraries and museums.

John D. Rockefeller was the leader of America's oil industry. His Standard Oil Company first grew by producing oil for paraffin lamps. Later, oil was used to make petrol for cars. Rockefeller, too, gave away about half a billion dollars.

Unions
Factories, steel **mills** and coal mines were dangerous places to work. Heavy machines, vats of melted steel and rock falls in underground mines killed many workers. The working week was 12 hours a day, six days a week. Two million children under age 15 worked liked this.

A single worker had little power to change things. Some leaders organized workers into **unions**. When a union of workers stopped working, or held a **strike**, the factory owner had problems.

▲ Mary Harris Jones organized workers to join unions, marches and strikes against poor working conditions, long hours and low wages. Here she is marching with child workers in 1910. But most strikes did not help workers get better treatment.

Women at work
By 1900, more than a million women worked in factories. Many unions did not let women join. However, in 1910, 20,000 women and men in clothing factories organized the International Ladies' Garment Workers Union. They held a strike for several weeks. Factory owners finally gave them better pay and shorter working hours.

▲ This photograph shows factories and mills in Pittsburgh in 1903. Smoke from furnaces in the steel mills caused air pollution.

▶ Inside the steel mill, machines melt iron, blow in cool air and turn the iron into steel. It was a hot, dangerous place to work.

MOVING FASTER

One visitor to New York City's Broadway street observed: "It takes more skill to cross Broadway... than to cross the Atlantic in a clamboat (rowing boat)." Delivery trucks, horse-drawn carriages, cars, walkers – they all jammed into city streets at the same time.

America expands
Three states join the nation, completing the 48 states on the mainland.
1907 Oklahoma
1912 New Mexico
1912 Arizona

Many cities hired tall police officers to control the traffic problems. The police wore white gloves and blew a whistle to hold back some vehicles and move along others. In 1914, Cleveland, Ohio, installed the nation's first electric traffic light. It was operated by a policeman standing in a nearby booth. In 1904, New York State passed a speed limit of 16 km per hour in busy cities.

◀▶ From 1903 to 1914, the United States built the Panama Canal in Central America. Ships could now travel between the Atlantic and Pacific Oceans without going around South America. It reduced the journey time from New York to San Francisco by more than half

◀ The Woolworth Building was completed in New York City in 1913. At 241.5 m, it became the tallest building in the world. (By comparison, Canary Wharf Tower in London is 244 m.)

Above and below the traffic

By the early 1900s, overhead electric trains operated in Chicago, Boston and New York City. They ran on tracks above the traffic. In 1904, the first underground, or subway, trains ran beneath New York City. Boston had had an underground railway since 1897.

In 1901, shoppers in Philadelphia experienced a new way to move. Gimbel's department store installed an escalator. From then on, all the big-city department stores installed these new moving staircases. Pavements were also changing. They were playgrounds where children played hopscotch. They were also markets where sellers on stalls offered everything from pans to pickles.

◀ By 1910, the centre of New York City was filled with all kinds of vehicles. People made their way across the cobbled streets, weaving among the traffic.

▼ This photograph from about 1900 shows the Jewish market on Hester Street in New York City.

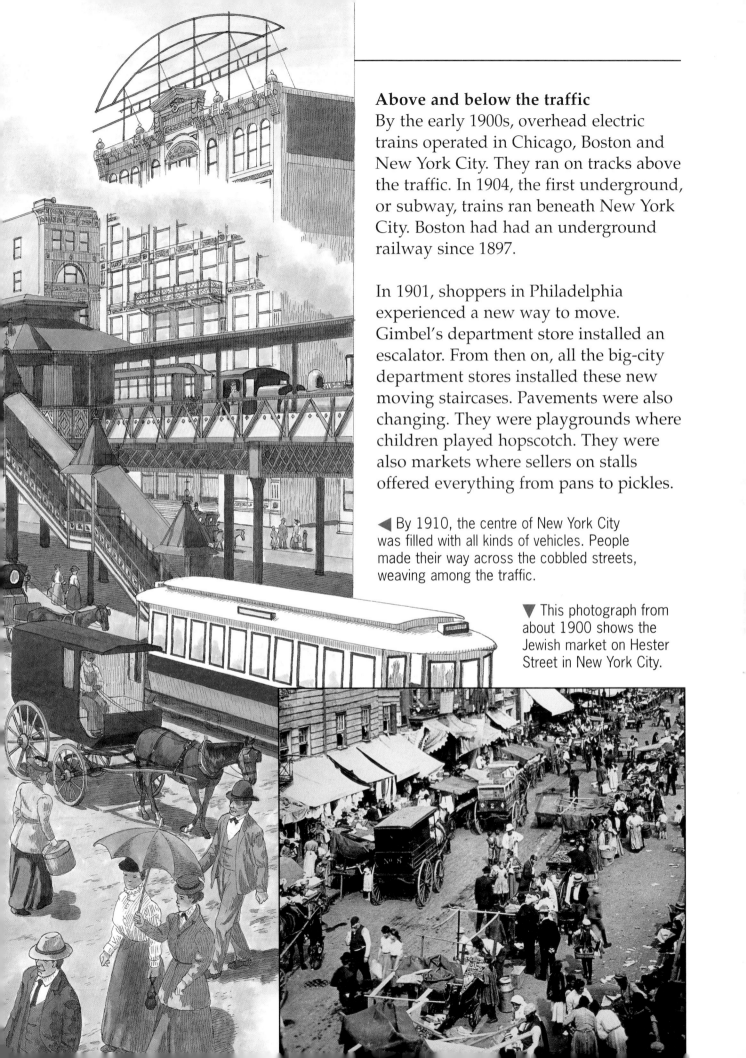

THE FIRST WORLD WAR

In 1914, war broke out in Europe. France, Italy, Russia and Britain were on the side called the Allied Powers. Germany, Turkey and Austria-Hungary were called the Central Powers. The war spread through Europe and then to Asia, Africa, the Middle East and the Pacific. It became the First World War.

When the war started, US President Woodrow Wilson assured everyone that the United States would not take sides. This became increasingly difficult. The German government began using its new submarines to launch torpedoes to sink Allied ships. On 7 May 1915, the Germans sank the British passenger ship *Lusitania*. Nearly 1200 people were killed, including 128 Americans.

By 1917, Germany was attacking US ships bringing supplies to Britain. On 2 April 1917, President Wilson asked **Congress** to declare war on Germany. By 6 April, Congress declared war and the United States entered the conflict.

Americans at war

Even before 1917, many Americans went to Europe and volunteered to fight for the Allies and work in their war hospitals. Once the United States officially joined the war, nearly five million Americans became soldiers, pilots, doctors and nurses. At first, the country was so short of guns that American soldiers did their training with broomsticks. Although short of supplies, the Americans brought plenty of energy to the battle-weary Allies.

▼ American soldiers went to war with worn-out guns. They said goodbye to their loved ones and boarded trains for New York and New Jersey. From there, they took ships across the Atlantic.

▲ An American soldier carrying his equipment.

► Women played an important role in the First World War. They joined the US armed forces and became nurses, radio operators and office assistants. This woman drove an ambulance in France. After the war, many Americans felt that women deserved the right to vote.

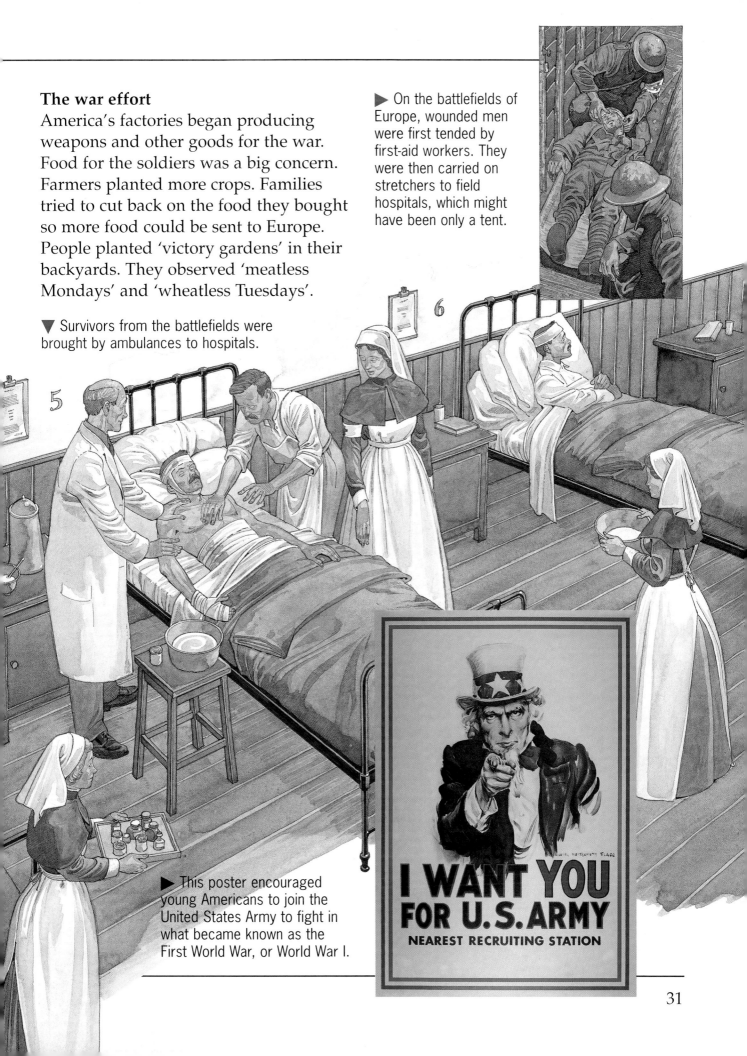

The war effort

America's factories began producing weapons and other goods for the war. Food for the soldiers was a big concern. Farmers planted more crops. Families tried to cut back on the food they bought so more food could be sent to Europe. People planted 'victory gardens' in their backyards. They observed 'meatless Mondays' and 'wheatless Tuesdays'.

▼ Survivors from the battlefields were brought by ambulances to hospitals.

▶ On the battlefields of Europe, wounded men were first tended by first-aid workers. They were then carried on stretchers to field hospitals, which might have been only a tent.

▶ This poster encouraged young Americans to join the United States Army to fight in what became known as the First World War, or World War I.

I WANT YOU FOR U.S. ARMY
NEAREST RECRUITING STATION

AMERICANS IN BATTLE

World War I was different from earlier wars. First, it was worldwide. Twenty-eight nations were at war. These nations spanned from China and Japan to Cuba and Panama. Battles were fought throughout Europe and the Middle East. Second, this war was fought with the most powerful and deadliest weapons yet.

For the first time, all armies used machine-guns against their enemies. In a few seconds, a soldier could fire hundreds of shots. In the first few months of the war, a million men were killed by machine-guns. Never before did armies have tanks, **grenades** or poison gas. This war took the lives of 10 million soldiers.

Battlefield in the sky
At the beginning of the war in 1914, aircraft were quite new. They were also slow and unreliable. They were mainly used to spy on the enemy. As countries built better planes, they used them to drop bombs. To drive these planes away, enemy pilots used machine-guns. These pilots were brave and daring. They flew alone, with no parachutes. When a plane was hit, it spun in flames to the ground.

On the ground
Most of the war was fought on the ground. The land was open and flat. Armies dug deep trenches to protect themselves against enemy attack. Soldiers stayed there for weeks at a time – eating, sleeping and hoping to stay alive.

▶ American soldiers take a needed rest in a trench in the Argonne Forest in France.

World War I
1914
28 July Austria-Hungary (Central Powers) declares war on Serbia (Allied Powers)
1–3 Aug. Germany (Central) declares war on Russia and France (Allied)
4 Aug. Britain (Allied) declares war on Germany
Aug. Japan (Allied) declares war on Germany
Nov. Allied Powers declare war on Ottoman Empire of Turkey (Central)
1915 Italy enters the war (Allied)
1917 US enters the war (Allied)
1918 war ends with Allied victory

▼ An American soldier receives help during fighting at Varennes, France. About 365,000 Americans were killed or wounded in the war.

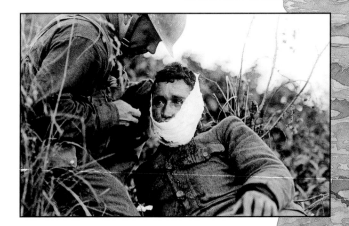

▶ The skies over Europe were ablaze with gunfire. An American-piloted fighter plane turns to attack a German plane. A burning plane falls to the ground.

The end of the war

On 11 November 1918, the weakened Central Powers asked to stop the fighting. America and the other Allies celebrated. World leaders, including US President Woodrow Wilson, met in France to sign a peace treaty. Germany had to pay for war damages and give up some of its land. Wilson hoped for world peace. But 21 years later, another world war began.

◀ Millions of women who had never worked before took jobs in the United States during the war. Many worked in factories making guns, uniforms and ammunition (as shown here). Others took over men's jobs driving tramcars. After the war, many women gave up their jobs to returning soldiers. Others kept on working in factories (as shown here), even though they earned less than men at the same jobs.

33

A Battle Against Disease

It was hard enough for Americans to live with a war in 1918. That year, another deadly enemy struck. It was a deadly virus people called Spanish influenza. It spread throughout the world. Doctors tried to control the disease, but there was little they could do.

The 1918 influenza killed 20 million people worldwide. More than half a million Americans died, mostly in large cities. The disease spread rapidly. Telephone and other services were not operating because so many workers were sick. Factories closed even though they were needed to produce goods for the war. Doctors warned people to stay away from crowds. In New York and Chicago, it was against the law to sneeze or cough in public without a handkerchief.

▶ Health workers rushed the very sick to hospitals. Everyone on the street had to wear masks to prevent spread of the germs. Some cities had $100 fines for not wearing them. Still, the disease spread rapidly for about nine months. Gradually, fewer people got sick and life returned to normal.

▶ Many hospitals were built in the United States in the 1910s. This is a photograph taken in about 1920 in a hospital in Minneapolis, Minnesota. Children suffering from the disease tuberculosis are receiving sun-baths on a day when it was too cold to sit outdoors – sunshine and fresh air ease the symptoms of the disease.

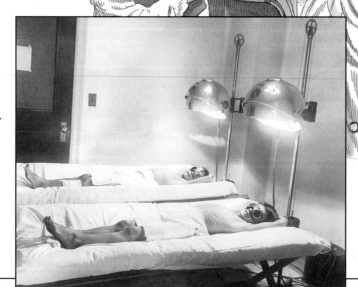

The US government did not want diseases coming into the country. When **immigrants** arrived at **Ellis Island**, they were examined by doctors. Anyone with a serious disease was sent back home.

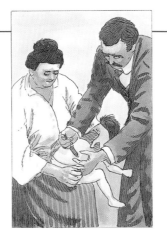

Vaccine shots can keep children from getting certain diseases. In the 1920s, doctors began vaccinating against **diphtheria**. A vaccine against smallpox had been given since 1796.

Early hospitals

Before the 1800s, mostly poor people went to hospitals. Hospitals were run by **charities**. Poor people had nowhere else to go when they got sick. When wealthy people got sick, they paid doctors to come to their houses and take care of them. America's first hospitals were dirty, crowded and dark. Patient beds were lined up in one big room. Diseases spread rapidly. Doctors did not know that cleanliness reduced infections.

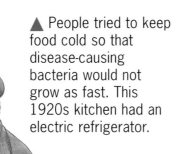

People tried to keep food cold so that disease-causing bacteria would not grow as fast. This 1920s kitchen had an electric refrigerator.

Improvements

In the late 1800s, hospitals grew more successful in controlling germs. Also, American nursing schools began training nurses to care for patients. Hospitals started to build private rooms for patients. New equipment and techniques for surgery were developed. By the early 1900s, most people felt that hospitals could help them get better.

Getting healthier	
mid-1800s Louis Pasteur discovers how to **pasteurize** milk and other foods to keep them from spoiling	**1895** Wilhelm Roentgen discovers X-rays
	1898 Pierre and Marie Curie discover radium as a powerful weapon against cancer
1865 Joseph Lister invents **antiseptic** to fight infections during surgery	**1920** Earl Dickson invents Band-Aids

PROHIBITION

There were 13 years in American history when it was illegal to make or sell alcoholic beverages. This was called Prohibition. When the 18th Amendment became law in 1920, it was a great victory for many groups that thought alcohol caused too many problems.

Drinking beer, rum and other liquor (alcohol) had been custom in America since colonial days. In the 1800s, many groups – including women's groups and churches – fought to make such drinking illegal. Drinking made people irresponsible, they argued. Drinking made people have poor judgement. Susan B. Anthony had spoken out against alcohol since the 1850s. Many states did become 'dry'. That means there was a law against buying or selling alcohol. Some people wanted to make alcoholic drinks illegal throughout the United States.

Changing the law

In 1917, **Congress** passed the 18th **Amendment**. In 1919, lawmakers in at least three-fourths, or 36, of the states approved the amendment. The **Prohibition** law went into effect in 1920. Bars and off-licences closed down throughout the country. People in favour of Prohibition celebrated. However, Prohibition was a failure. Many Americans still drank – illegally.

▲▼ Illegal alcohol could be bought at a speakeasy. Paul Morand, a French author, visited New York in the 1920s and wrote: "Some speakeasies are disguised as florists' shops, or behind undertakers' coffins. The door is closed and is only opened after you have been scrutinized (looked at) through a door-catch or barred opening. They are popular in all classes of society; women go there gladly."

▲ Federal agents dismantle an illegal alcohol still.

By 1928, over 80 million people went to the cinema each week. They paid 10 or 15 cents to laugh at Charlie Chaplin and Buster Keaton, or thrill to the cowboy adventures of Tom Mix or Thomas Hart (right).

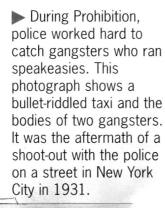

During Prohibition, police worked hard to catch gangsters who ran speakeasies. This photograph shows a bullet-riddled taxi and the bodies of two gangsters. It was the aftermath of a shoot-out with the police on a street in New York City in 1931.

Life during Prohibition

People called bootleggers brought in illegal alcohol from Canada and the Caribbean Islands. Illegal bars, called speakeasies, opened. Gangsters took over the sale of illegal alcohol. They forced speakeasy owners to buy from them.

Every day, millions of Americans broke the law to buy alcohol. People began asking: "What good is a law that is constantly broken? Shouldn't people have the right to choose to drink?" On 5 December 1933, the 21st Amendment was passed. It cancelled Prohibition.

A VICTORY FOR WOMEN

Thousands of women helped the nation survive World War I. On 30 September 1918, President Woodrow Wilson spoke to Congress about this: "We have made partners of the women in this war; shall we admit them only to a partnership of suffering and . . . not to a partnership of privilege and right?"

During the war, women had nursed soldiers, raised money and operated factory machines. How could they still be denied a voice in America's government? Throughout the war, two **suffrage** leaders led marches in Washington DC. Alice Paul and Lucy Burns had begun their **protest** marches in 1912. Day after day, groups of women marched around the White House. In June 1917, police arrested the women and charged them with blocking traffic. The women were given a choice of a $25 fine or three days in jail. The women chose jail.

▲ Women held jobs in government offices, schools, hospitals and stores. By 1920, it was hard to argue that women were not smart enough to vote.

Why not let them vote?

Many people who opposed suffrage earned money making and selling alcohol. They thought that if women got the right to vote, they would vote for **Prohibition**. As it turned out, Prohibition passed even without the women's vote.

Some people felt women were not ready to vote. Even some women did not want to be involved in the 'dirty business of politics'. Former President William Howard Taft wrote an article saying that women had a 'lack of experience' and an 'excess of emotion' which would prevent them from making wise decisions. Despite these arguments, the Anthony **Amendment** became the 19th Amendment to the **Constitution** on 26 August 1920. Women in the United States finally had the right to vote.

GIVE YOUR CHILDREN EQUAL RIGHTS
VOTE YES Nov. 2
On the AMENDMENT ENABLING WOMAN TO VOTE
MASSACHUSETTS WOMAN SUFFRAGE ASSOCIATION
585 BOYLSTON ST., BOSTON, MASS.
TERESA CROWLEY
GERTRUDE HALLADAY LEONARD

▲ A 1915 poster for women's votes.

Anthony Amendment
1878 the Amendment is presented to Congress, but fails to be accepted
4 June 1919 House of Representatives and the **Senate** approve the amendment
18 August 1920 Tennessee lawmakers approve the amendment, making it the 36th – and last – state needed to approve it
26 August 1920 President Wilson signs the law
November 1920 26 million women – half of those who could – vote

▶ ▼ Like millions of other women, these women in New York City are demonstrating for their right to vote. Carrie Chapman Catt, who fought hard for the vote said: "Women have suffered an agony of soul . . . that you and your daughters might **inherit** political freedom. That vote has been costly. Prize it!"

VOTE

WOMEN'S
VOTE
NOW

WOMEN'S
SUFFRAG

MR. PRESIDENT
HOW LONG
MUST
WOMEN WAIT
FOR LIBERTY

VO
NO

THE ROARING TWENTIES

For the first time in history, people could hear the presidential election results on the radio. It was 2 November 1920. Over the next ten years, American families bought new cars. Women started wearing dresses that showed their legs. Charles Lindbergh flew alone across the Atlantic Ocean.

▼ George Herman Ruth was known as Babe Ruth. He played baseball for the New York Yankees. Before 1920, the home run record for one season was 27. That year Ruth hit 54. His season-best was 60.

Many people say that the 1920s were the beginning of modern times. Radios, cars, cinema and flight all became popular. For the first time, more Americans lived in cities than on farms. Americans were making more goods and more money than ever. There seemed to be jobs for everyone, and everyone was having fun. It was a reaction against the miseries of war. For all these reasons, the 1920s were nicknamed the 'Roaring Twenties'.

Many new products became available in the 1920s. Washing machines, vacuum cleaners and refrigerators made housework easier. Women had more freedom to take jobs outside the home, attend university and participate in politics and government.

In 1924, more than five million people owned radios. In 1927, you could watch a film and hear the actors talk! In 1928, a young film-maker named Walt Disney produced the first movie cartoon. It was called *Steamboat Willie* and starred Mickey Mouse.

► During the Roaring Twenties, people went to nightclubs to eat, listen to music and dance. The latest dance was called the Charleston.

Daring fashions

Before the 1920s, women made sure to cover their ankles with long skirts and high-top shoes. Women in the 1920s dared to change. They began to wear short dresses and stockings rolled down to the knee. Modern women 'bobbed' their hair. That means they cut it short. It was even acceptable to wear makeup, such as lipstick, rouge (blush) and powder.

▼ A new kind of music, called jazz, became popular in the Roaring Twenties. This is Joe 'King' Oliver's Creole Jazz Band. Many jazz musicians were and still are African American. Jazz is a combination of African rhythms and European-style instruments. Musicians in New Orleans and Chicago started playing jazz music. It became popular all over the world. During the Roaring Twenties, musicians played jazz in nightclubs where people could dance all night.

Historical Map of America

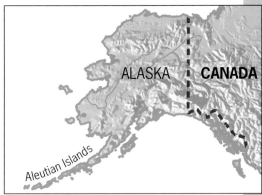

ALASKA | CANADA

Aleutian Islands

On the map

By 1928, there were 48 states in the United States. The entire mainland had been divided into states. Cities had grown up across the nation, but especially along the East and West Coasts and around the Great Lakes. The cities were linked by an extensive railway network. Mostly in the West, a number of national parks had been set up to protect areas of natural beauty from development. The last remaining Native American groups lived on **reservations** throughout the **Great Plains** and West.

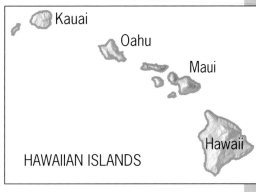

Kauai

Oahu

Maui

Hawaii

HAWAIIAN ISLANDS

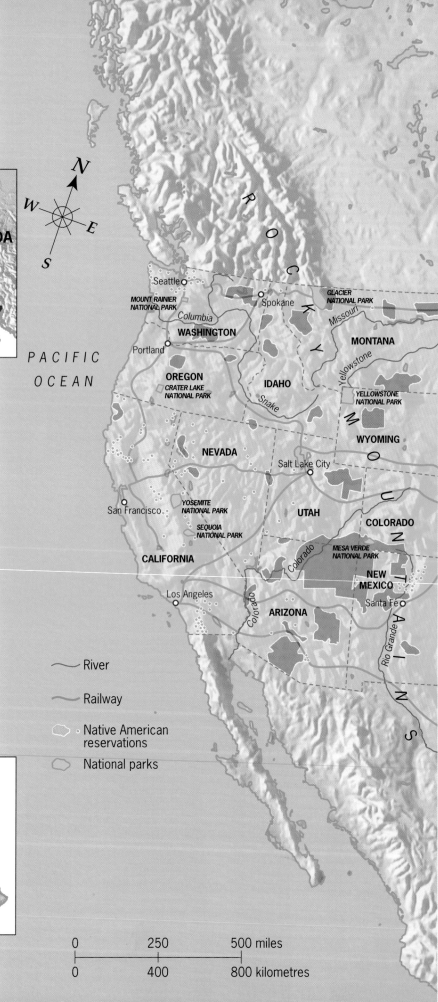

PACIFIC OCEAN

Seattle
MOUNT RAINIER NATIONAL PARK
Spokane
Columbia
GLACIER NATIONAL PARK
Missouri
WASHINGTON
Portland
MONTANA
OREGON
CRATER LAKE NATIONAL PARK
IDAHO
Yellowstone
Snake
YELLOWSTONE NATIONAL PARK
WYOMING
NEVADA
Salt Lake City
R O C K Y
San Francisco
YOSEMITE NATIONAL PARK
SEQUOIA NATIONAL PARK
UTAH
COLORADO
M O U N T A I N S
Colorado
MESA VERDE NATIONAL PARK
CALIFORNIA
NEW MEXICO
Los Angeles
Colorado
ARIZONA
Santa Fe
Rio Grande

River

Railway

Native American reservations

National parks

0   250   500 miles
0   400   800 kilometres

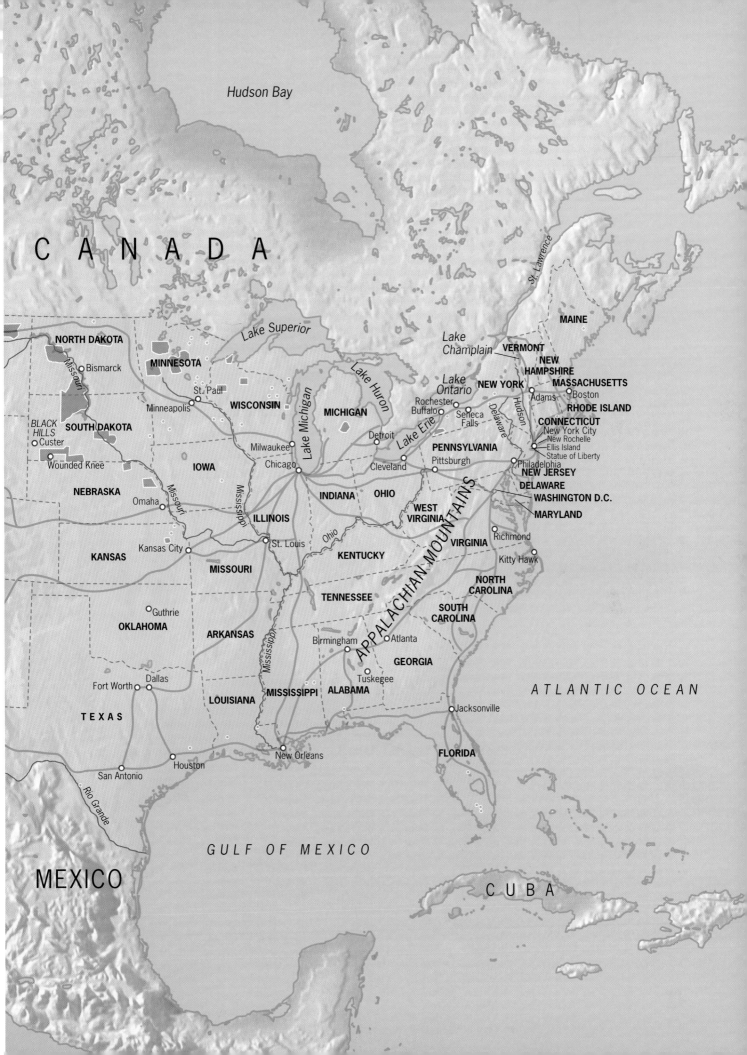

Hudson Bay

C A N A D A

Lake Superior

NORTH DAKOTA
Bismarck

MINNESOTA

St. Paul

Minneapolis

WISCONSIN

Milwaukee

Lake Michigan

MICHIGAN

Lake Huron

Detroit

Lake Erie

Lake
Ontario

Rochester
Buffalo

Lake
Champlain

MAINE

VERMONT
NEW
HAMPSHIRE

NEW YORK

MASSACHUSETTS
Adams   Boston

RHODE ISLAND

Seneca
Falls

St. Lawrence

Hudson

Delaware

CONNECTICUT
New York City
New Rochelle
Ellis Island
Statue of Liberty

Philadelphia

NEW JERSEY

DELAWARE

WASHINGTON D.C.

MARYLAND

BLACK
HILLS
Custer

SOUTH DAKOTA

Wounded Knee

Missouri

IOWA

Chicago

ILLINOIS

St. Louis

INDIANA

OHIO

Cleveland

PENNSYLVANIA

Pittsburgh

WEST
VIRGINIA

VIRGINIA

Richmond

Kitty Hawk

NEBRASKA

Omaha

Missouri

Mississippi

Ohio

KENTUCKY

APPALACHIAN MOUNTAINS

KANSAS

Kansas City

MISSOURI

TENNESSEE

NORTH
CAROLINA

SOUTH
CAROLINA

Guthrie

OKLAHOMA

ARKANSAS

Birmingham

Atlanta

GEORGIA

Tuskegee

Mississippi

Fort Worth   Dallas

LOUISIANA

MISSISSIPPI

ALABAMA

Jacksonville

ATLANTIC OCEAN

TEXAS

New Orleans

Houston

FLORIDA

San Antonio

Rio Grande

GULF OF MEXICO

MEXICO

CUBA

FAMOUS PEOPLE OF THE TIME

Jane Addams,
1860–1935, founded Hull House in Chicago to help poor people. She shared the Nobel Peace Prize in 1931.

Susan Brownell Anthony,
1820–1906, helped organize the women's movement that first changed New York's property ownership laws and later won nationwide women's voting rights.

Andrew Carnegie,
1835–1919, owned iron mines, ships and railways. By 1900, his company made a quarter of all the steel in the US.

George Washington Carver,
1864?–1943, was an African American chemist who worked to improve the farm economy of the South. He discovered hundreds of uses for peanuts, sweet potatoes and soybeans.

Carrie Chapman Catt,
1859–1947, became a leader of the women's suffrage movement.

Frederick Douglass,
1817–1895, escaped slavery and started an anti-slavery newspaper in Rochester, New York State.

Thomas Edison,
1847–1931, was one of the greatest inventors in history. His work helped bring electric lights, phonographs and motion pictures to people around the world.

Henry Ford,
1863–1947, started the Ford Motor Company in 1903. He created the assembly-line system, which built cars faster and cheaper.

Benjamin Harrison,
1833–1901, was the 23rd US president. He insisted that the America flag be flown above the White House, other government buildings and every school in the country.

Andrew Johnson,
1808–1875, was the 17th US president. He was impeached by the House of Representatives. Many disapproved of his generosity to the South after the Civil War. The Senate voted to keep him in office.

Mary Harris Jones,
1830–1930, helped organize trade unions in the early 1900s. Most workers called her 'Mother Jones'.

Abraham Lincoln,
1809–1865, was the 16th US president. In 1863, he moved to end slavery with the Emancipation Proclamation. During the Civil War, his main goal was to preserve the Union.

Lucretia Mott,
1793–1880, fought against slavery, alcohol and unfair treatment of workers. She was a leader in the women's suffrage movement. She helped organize the first women's rights convention at Seneca Falls, New York.

IMPORTANT DATES AND EVENTS

SUSAN B. ANTHONY
1820 born in Adams, Massachusetts, on 15 February
1826 moves to New York State
1840 works as a teacher in a boarding school in New Rochelle, New York State
1846–1849 works as headmistress at Canajoharie Academy
1848 the first women's rights convention is held at Seneca Falls
1851 meets Elizabeth Cady Stanton
1852 organizes the Women's State Temperance Society with Stanton
1856 serves as the New York State agent for the Anti-slavery Society
1860 convinces New York lawmakers to pass the Married Woman's Property Act
1868–1870 publishes the *Revolution* newspaper with Stanton
1869 starts the National Woman Suffrage Association with Stanton
1872 is arrested for voting illegally
1878 the Anthony Amendment is introduced into Congress
1906 dies of pneumonia on 13 March

OTHER EVENTS IN THE UNITED STATES 1845 to 1886
1845 Texas and Florida become states
1846 Iowa becomes a state
1848 Oregon becomes part of the US
1846–1848 US–Mexican War
1848 Wisconsin becomes a state
1848 California gold rush begins
1850 California becomes a state
1851 Fort Laramie Treaty promises Native Americans money and food for land
1858 Minnesota becomes a state
1859 Oregon becomes a state
1861 Kansas becomes a state
1861 Abraham Lincoln becomes president
1861 Civil War begins
1862 Homestead Act opens Great Plains land to settlers
1863 Emancipation Proclamation frees slaves in Confederate states
1863 West Virginia becomes a state
1864 Nevada becomes a state
1865 13th Amendment ends slavery
1865 Civil War ends
1865 President Lincoln is assassinated
1867 Nebraska becomes a state
1867 US buys Alaska from Russia
1868 House of Representatives impeaches President Johnson; Senate acquits him
1868 14th Amendment guarantees citizenship rights to all people born in the US
1869 the transcontinental railway is completed
1876 America celebrates its 100th birthday
1876 Colorado becomes a state
1877 Chief Joseph of the Nez Perce surrenders and takes his people to a reservation
1881 Sitting Bull surrenders for his Sioux people
1886 Geronimo and the Apache surrender and move to a reservation

John D. Rockefeller, 1837–1937, organized the Standard Oil Company in 1870. He bought companies and merged with his competitors until he controlled almost all of the oil refining in the US In 1911, the Supreme Court ordered the large company to break into smaller companies.

Theodore Roosevelt, 1858–1919, was a hero in the Spanish–American War. In 1901, he was vice-president when President McKinley was assassinated. He served as president from 1901 to 1909. He favoured conservation of the country's natural beauty and created the National Forest Service.

Elizabeth Cady Stanton, 1815–1902, led the women's movement with Susan B. Anthony. She organized the first women's rights convention at Seneca Falls, New York, with Lucretia Mott. Susan B. Anthony did not attend this meeting.

Mark Twain (real name Samuel Clemens), 1835–1910, was an American adventurer and writer. In 1873, he wrote *The Gilded Age*, making fun of the selfishness and money-making schemes of the time. Later, he wrote his most famous books, *The Adventures of Tom Sawyer* and *The Adventures of Huckleberry Finn*.

Booker T. Washington, 1856–1915, directed the Tuskegee Institute in Alabama and turned it into one of the leading schools for African Americans. He thought African Americans should get education and work skills before they could demand equal treatment. Other African-American leaders criticized him for this.

Victoria Woodhull, 1838–1937, was a newspaper writer who wrote about women's suffrage. In 1872, she was the first female candidate for president. She ran for the small People's Party. In 1871, she was the first woman to speak before the US Congress about women's rights.

Orville Wright, 1871–1948, and **Wilbur Wright,** 1867–1912, were America's best-known aeroplane inventors. On 17 December 1903, they made the first four sustained flights in a power-driven aeroplane.

US presidents from 1845 to 1928

James Knox Polk 1845–1849
Zachary Taylor 1849–1850
Millard Fillmore 1850–1853
Franklin Pierce 1853–1857
James Buchanan 1857–1861
Abraham Lincoln 1861–1865
Andrew Johnson 1865–1869
Ulysses S. Grant 1869–1877
Rutherford B. Hayes 1877–1881
James A. Garfield 1881–1881
Chester A. Arthur 1881–1885
Grover Cleveland 1885–1889; 1893–1897
Benjamin Harrison 1889–1893
William McKinley 1897–1901
Theodore Roosevelt 1901-1909
William Howard Taft 1909-1913
Woodrow Wilson 1913-1921
Warren G. Harding 1921-1923
Calvin Coolidge 1923-1929

OTHER EVENTS IN THE US 1886 to 1928
1881 James Garfield is assassinated
1886 Statue of Liberty, a gift from France, is completed
1889 North Dakota, South Dakota, Washington and Montana become states
1889 former Native American land in Oklahoma is open for settlers
1890 Wyoming is granted statehood and becomes the first state to allow women to vote
1898 Spanish–American War; US takes over the Philippines, Puerto Rico and the island of Guam
1900 US establishes Territory of Hawaii
1901 President McKinley is assassinated
1907 Oklahoma becomes a state
1912 New Mexico and Arizona become states
1914 the Panama Canal is completed
1914 World War I begins in Europe
1917 US enters World War I
1917 Prohibition begins with the 18th Amendment
1918 World War I ends
1920 Women win the right to vote with the 19th Amendment

THE REST OF NORTH AND SOUTH AMERICA
1846–1848 US–Mexican War. Mexico loses California, Arizona, New Mexico, Utah, Colorado
1867 Canada granted self-government by Britain
1868–1878 Cuba loses war of independence against Spain
1877 Rise of dictator Porfirio Diaz in Mexico. He stays in power until 1911.
1879 Chile at war with Bolivia (until 1883) and with Peru (until 1884). Chile victorious in both wars and gains much land.
1889 Brazil becomes a republic
1910 civil war in Mexico

THE REST OF THE WORLD
1845 potato famine in Ireland
1848 revolutions in Italy, France, Austria and Germany
1854 US forces Japan to open its ports to Western trade
1854–1856 Crimean War – France and Britain help Turkey against Russia
1863 start of French empire in Indo-China
1869 Suez Canal is opened
1870 Franco–Prussian War: France defeated
1870–1899 Britain, France, Italy, Germany, Belgium, Spain and Portugal set up colonies in Africa
1910 China abolishes slavery
1914–1918 World War I
1917 Russian Revolution
1922 Soviet states form the USSR; Mussolini forms Fascist government in Italy
1923 Adolf Hitler organizes the Nazi Party in Germany

GLOSSARY

amendment change in a document, such as the US Constitution

antiseptic something that kills germs and prevents infection

anti-slavery opposing slavery (someone owning another person)

bail money paid to a court to allow someone accused of a crime to be set free until the trial

charity help given to people in need

Civil War in the US, fighting between northern and southern states from 1861 to 1865

claim to establish or say that something belongs to you

Congress part of the US government that makes laws

constitution set of laws that state the rights of the people and the powers of government

convention a meeting

cooperative working together for a common purpose

diphtheria serious infection of the lungs or skin

election process of choosing someone by voting

Ellis Island island in New York Harbour with buildings used to receive and inspect people who entered the United States from other countries

Great Plains enormous area of flat grassland between the Mississippi River and the Rocky Mountains

grenade small bomb that is thrown by hand or fired from a rifle

House of Representatives one of two parts of the US government that makes laws; part of Congress

immigrant someone who arrives from another country

inherit to receive money or property from someone who dies

mill factory for making products such as cloth, paper and steel

Panama Canal waterway that cuts across the country of Panama and connects the Atlantic and Pacific Oceans

pasteurize to heat milk or other liquid enough to kill harmful bacteria

petition letter signed by many people asking those in power to change the law or take other action

pioneer person who does something first to make it easier for others to follow

Prohibition period from 1920 to 1933 when it was illegal to make or sell alcoholic beverages

property anything owned by an individual

protest to object to something publicly

reservation area of land set aside by the government for a special purpose, such as a place for Native Americans to live

revolution important change, such as changing the system of government or changing the way people live

Senate one of two parts of the US government that makes laws; part of Congress

settlement house place where immigrants and poor people went for help

settler person who makes a home in a new place

slave person who is owned by another person and is usually made to work for that person without pay

strike refuse to work because of a disagreement with an employer

suffrage right to vote

Supreme Court highest court in the United States, having the power to overturn decisions made in lower courts

temperance movement people who wanted to outlaw alcoholic beverages

tenement run-down apartment building

territory in the US, an area of land that is not yet a state

union group of workers who join together to try to improve working conditions, wages and benefits

vaccine substance given to a person, as an injection or by mouth, to protect him or her from disease

MORE BOOKS TO READ

To Kill a Mocking Bird. Harper Lee, Heinemann.

Black Settlers in Britain 1555-1958. N. File and C. Power, Heinemann.

Slavery from Africa to the Americas. C. Hatt, Evans.

Tell Me About Emmeline Pankhurst. M. Pollard, Evans.

Women in 19th-Century America. F. Macdonald, Belitha Press.

Living Through History: Britain 1750-1900. N. Kelly, R. Rees, J. Shuter, Heinemann.

PLACES TO VISIT

The American Museum in Britain
Claverton Manor
Bath BA2 7BD
Tel: 01225 460 503

Merseyside Maritime Museum
Albert Dock
Liverpool L3 4AQ
Tel: 0151 478 4499

Institute for Race Relations
2-6 Leeke Street
London WC1X 9HS
Tel: 020 7837 0041

Fawcett Society Library
London Guildhall University
Old Castle Street
London E1 7NT
Tel: 020 7320 1189

INDEX

INDEX